Women
STANDING WITH THEIR
MEN

JOYCE LESTER

J.L. Ministries
St. Paul, MN

WOMEN STANDING WITH THEIR MEN

© 2006 by Joyce Lester

A production of

J.L. Ministries

P.O. Box 65210   St. Paul, MN 55165
Tel: (612-203-7603)
E-mail: jlm@joycelester.org
Website: joycelester.org

Editor: Les Lester, MA (abt)
Cover Design: Promise Amajiri

This book or parts thereof may not be reproduced in any form, stored in a retrieval system, or transmitted in any form by any means, electronic, mechanical, photocopy, recording, or otherwise, without prior written permission of the publisher, except as provided by United States of America copyright law.

All scriptural quotations are from the King James Version of the Bible

ISBN 0-9768680-6-7

Published in the United States of America by

burningbush creation

DEDICATION

To all the wives who are standing in the gap for their families, I salute you. My prayer is that the principles in this book will enlighten, encourage and inspire you to continue your spiritual fight for your husbands, your children and yourself.

To my loving husband, Les, who was placed in my life 18 years ago, and who has always encouraged me and given me the freedom to soar like an eagle, to pursue and fulfill my God-given destiny.

To my mother and father, who were married for 48 years and are now with the Lord. I thank God for my mother who refused to stop praying for my father to be saved. She continually prayed for him for over 25 years.

To my dear friend and spiritual mentor Yvonne Moody, who has counseled, encouraged and prayed for me for over 30 years, I thank you from the depths of my heart.

To my two lovely daughters Alisha and Shiree, I thank God for having you in my life.

To Pastor Geraldine Dozier, a true example of the Proverbs 31 woman and a role model to women on how to be their husband's cheerleader. And to her loving husband, Apostle Bennie Dozier, who saw the call on my life and spoke into my life, many times, what God had revealed He was going to do in me.

J.L. Ministries

Joyce Lester is available for:

Conferences
Workshops
Seminars
Revivals

For bookings call 612/203-7603, or email your request to jlm@joycelester.org.

Women Standing With Their Men Q & A

If you have **marital issues, which reflect the topic of this book**, and you would like to ask Joyce a question, you may do so by visiting her website at

www.joycelester.org

Contents

Introduction

Chapter One	Wrong Enemy
Chapter Two	The Power in a godly Woman
Chapter Three	Standing by Our Men
Chapter Four	Understanding Our Men
Chapter Five	A Helper
Chapter Six	A Spirit-Filled Home
Chapter Seven	Balanced Power
Chapter Eight	Hurt People, Hurt People
Chapter Nine	Are Your Wounds Healed?
Chapter Ten	Are You Expecting the Person Who Hurt You to Heal You?
Chapter Eleven	A Wise Woman Builds Her House
Chapter Twelve	Rebellion Brings Curses, Submission Brings Blessings

INTRODUCTION

It is important that Christian women keep the proper perspective in accordance with what God's Word says to wives. When talking to Christian women I have found that many have adopted the world's view as it relates to their roles as spouses. I have written this book to address the role of Christian wives, based on God's Word.

Satan has used the Women's Liberation Movement's beliefs and teachings to convince Christian women that they must stand up for their rights in the way the world does. He uses the philosophy of the organization to tell women they are justified in being angry and combative because of unfair treatment by men. The movement advocates that women are completely capable of living independent of men and no longer have to submit to their abuse and unfairness, in any area of their lives. No woman should tolerate abuse, but Satan has used the teachings of the movement to, in many ways, destabilize relationships between men and women.

The Women's Liberation Movement was originally intended to be an organized effort to obtain fair treatment politically and socially for females. The reason these women felt it necessary to establish the initiative was due to centuries of male-dominated society interpreting the role of the woman as subservient. Men were indoctrinated to subjugate women and treat them as objects of ownership. They believed the primary role of the woman was to bear children and please her husband.

The scriptures are clear on God's intent from the beginning, when He created man and woman; God's plan was for them to complement each other and work together. "And God said, Let us make man in our image, after our likeness: and let them have dominion over the fish of the sea, and over

Introduction cont.

the fowl of the air, and over the cattle, and over all the earth, and over every creeping thing that creepeth upon the earth. So God created man in his own image, in the image of God created he him; male and female created he them. And God blessed them, and God said unto them, Be fruitful, and multiply, and replenish the earth, and subdue it: and have dominion over the fish of the sea, and over the fowl of the air, and over every living thing that moveth upon the earth." (Genesis 1:26-28 KJV). It is clear in this passage of scripture that God's plan was always for man and woman to work in partnership in ruling over His creation.

God wants men and women to love and respect one another in the roles He designated for them. Neither role is more important than the other. An example of this is seen in procreation. In order to accomplish God's command to "be fruitful and multiply" both man and woman are necessary. Even though scientists have attempted to manipulate this process through invetro fertilization, via a test tube, it is not what God originally intended. Whenever we deviate from God's original intent, we fail to get God's best. God doesn't need us to try to improve on what He has done. We simply need to obey His Word, because God has the master plan. Our responsibility is to follow it according to the leading of His Holy Spirit. It is important that Christian wives keep the proper perspective in accordance with what God's Word says about us.

This book will give Christian wives instruction on how to stand with their husbands, how to strengthen their relationships, and how to set a proper example for their children to follow. Christian women should not be modeling their marriages after women in the world. Instead, we should follow the Bible which is God's manual for Christian living.

MEN AND WOMEN HAVE A COMMON ENEMY, *HIS NAME IS SATAN*

ONE

WRONG ENEMY

The Women's Liberation Movement was originally intended to be an organized effort to obtain fair and equal treatment politically and socially for women. Women grew tired of men who would not allow them to use their talents and creativity outside of the home. Some men would even make statements such as, "A woman's place is in the kitchen, to please her husband, and to take care of the children." Women who did not fit into this mold were considered either loose or rebellious. And even for those women who were able to venture into the workplace, it was understood that they were never to expect equal pay for equal work. Therefore, many women grew angry and frustrated by these inequities.

For centuries men misconstrued their role of authority in relationship to women. Their primary attitude was to subjugate a woman and make sure that she understood that he was in charge. In a male-dominated society women were thought of as objects for men's use, and sadly, women were not respected for their many contributions to society.

There are multitudes of women who have been hurt mentally, physically and emotionally by men. These women have pain and scars that make it difficult to trust or be committed to a man. Many times, the pain is so deep that it's hard to consider that, ultimately, Satan is the one who influences men to mistreat women. It is important that we not lose sight of the fact that Satan is always at the root of negative behavior, be it directly or indirectly.

Too many women are walking around with bitterness and unforgiveness festering inside of them. I have talked to women who said they had been sexually molested by men, beaten unmercifully and some said their husbands were in one or more affairs. One husband was caught up in pornography and no longer desired his wife. Some women said they were molested as children. One woman lost her husband to another man. I've heard numerous other painful and hideous stories from wives hurt by their husbands. These kinds of experiences create deep wounds and build walls within women, making it difficult to believe that their husband is not the real enemy.

In order for hurting women to be healed from their pain, they must be willing to forgive the men who hurt them, and remember that it is Satan who influences people to commit sinful acts against others. As long as women view the man as their adversary, they will be fighting the WRONG ENEMY! And that is exactly what Satan wants us to do because he knows this kind of attitude will keep women locked in their mental and emotional prisons. Forgiveness does not mean that someone is getting away with anything, because forgiveness does not erase

Wrong Enemy

consequences. God said "vengeance is mine." Therefore, we don't have to punish anyone for hurting us, because God's Law of sowing and reaping will take care of that.

The Women's Liberation Movement has greatly influenced the way women in today's society view themselves. There are television commercials, movies, talk shows, situation comedies, dating shows, etc. that promote the message of women being independent, in control and aggressive. They are told they no longer have to wait for a man to pursue them, but instead it is appropriate for the woman to chase the man. The idea of a woman who is ladylike, gentle, humble, submissive, sweet and nurturing is discouraged. Subsequently, these women are viewed as weak and out of touch with themselves.

The numbers of divorces and single-parent homes is rising, while same-sex relationships are increasing. Most people who are in same-sex relationships have been deeply wounded and disappointed as a result of some painful experience. Satan capitalizes on this hurt to promote division between men and women. Our children are confused, because they are receiving mixed messages about what a "normal" relationship should look like. As Christian women, it is crucial that we model what God deems as "normal" and appropriate. If we allow political correctness to dictate our standards of right and wrong, our children are doomed! That is why Christian women must view everything from God's eyes, a perspective which is found in His Word, and allow the Holy Spirit to give us wisdom and understanding of God's will.

Women are in competition with men on a daily basis for jobs, promotions and recognition. There are numerous marriages where both spouses are employed, and in many instances the wife's salary either matches or exceeds that of her husband. And unfortunately, there are more and more instances where the wife is working and is the only source of financial support for the family, because the husband is unemployed for one reason or another. As societal norms have changed, it has often impacted male and female relationships negatively. It has caused men and women to become angry and bitter towards one another. In today's society, the humanist philosophy is; "Make sure you take care of yourself first." If we do not keep our focus on God's Word and His perfect will, it is easy to adapt to the world's way of thinking.

Scripture tells us clearly, "We fight not against flesh and blood, but against principalities, powers and wickedness in high places." But Satan uses every opportunity, he gets, to convince us to fight each other. When we view humans as our enemy, Satan goes unchallenged in his efforts to destroy mankind, because we are too distracted with fighting one another.

As godly women, we must not allow the social and financial climate, of this world, to distract us or cause us to forget God's divine plan for men and women. When God created male and female, He said that they were to work together here on earth and subdue it together. Men and women have a common enemy, who is Satan. When they view one another as the enemy and fight each other, they are fighting the WRONG ENEMY. It is crucial that they work together to fight Satan, who loves to use his 'divide and conquer' strategy. Jesus warned Christians that a house divided cannot stand. Men and women are being influenced by the spirit of division on their jobs, in their homes and even in the Church. As a woman co-pastor I have often witnessed the bitterness and division between male and female ministers. Some women ministers, who have been rejected by men that do not believe God uses women in the ministry, don't realize the devil is using them to bring division and strife in the body of Christ. The Bible tells us, "Your gift will make room for you." Therefore, women should not allow the devil to get them into strife and out of God's will. There are enough unsaved people in this world that we will never run out of those who need the gospel. And God has enough male ministers, that do believe in women ministers, who will welcome women into their pulpits. You just need to pray and ask God to lead you to them. I love all of my co-laborers in the gospel, including the men who do not believe in woman ministers. Surely, there won't be a male and female heaven!

Principle # 1

Your husband is never your enemy; Satan is!

DEBORAH WAS PLACED at THE HEIGHT OF POLITICAL POWER

TWO

THE POWER IN A GODLY WOMAN

There were godly women who were in the forefront even during the Old Testament era. During that period, even though women were considered second class, or no class, with men dominating every area of society, God often used women. Some of the women in the Bible God used were Sarah, Miriam, Rahab, Ruth, Esther, Lydia, Priscilla, Anna, and of course Mary the mother of Jesus. These are just a few examples of powerful godly women. As Christian women, we sometimes lose sight of how powerful we are when we allow God to control our lives.

Deborah is an example of a woman who was very active in social and political issues, and she trusted God to lead her in how to operate in her position of authority.

DEBORAH

The only woman in the Bible who was placed at the height of political power by the common consent of the people was Deborah. Though she lived in the time of the Judges some thirteen centuries before Christ, there are few women in history who have ever attained the public dignity of Deborah. In all her roles, first that of counselor to her people, next as judge in their disputes, and finally as deliverer in time of war, Deborah exhibited womanly excellence. She was indeed "a mother in Israel." She rose to great leadership because she trusted God thoroughly in her heart and because she could inspire in others that same trust.

Long before Deborah became a leader in war, she was a homemaker. She would sit and give counsel to the people who came to her. As a counselor in time of peace, Deborah became known far and wide, but her greatest service came in time of war. She led her people into war. Most of them had stood by fearfully because they were afraid of the enemy's 900 chariots of iron, when they had none. While they fainted with fear, Deborah burned with indignation at the oppression of her people. You can find this and many more facts about Deborah and other women in the Bible, in All of The Women of the Bible, by Deen (Harper & Row Publisher).

Deborah is a wonderful model of godliness, wisdom, strength and power for Christian women. Her home was her first order of business. But she also allowed God to use her in her community, and ultimately in war. Barak, the Soldier was faint-hearted because he knew in the natural they were severely outnumbered, outpowered and unprepared to fight such a brutal enemy as Sisera, commander of Jabin's army. She convinced Barak that God, who had proven himself to be mightier than Pharoah, was mightier than their enemy. Deborah even gave Barak counsel as to how many troops

The Power In A Godly Woman

to take. But Barak refused to go without her because he recognized he needed her spiritual counsel along the way. Without hesitation Deborah said she would surely go with him. Deborah did not want any credit for herself, instead she wanted all the glory to be given to God. She knew that only God could bring them through the battle. Deborah also recognized and respected God's delegated authority. Therefore, she agreed to go with Barak and be by his side, but she wouldn't leave him and just take over.

It is important, as women of God, when we see situations where our husbands are abdicating their responsibilities as leaders, or if they are reticent that we don't just step in and take over. Instead, we should begin to pray for God to give us divine wisdom in how to assist and encourage our men to walk in the role God has set forth for them.

Many men have personal and emotional problems that hinder them from operating in their God-given role as leaders. Most men do not see themselves as God sees them. They often are not as willing as women to admit they are hurting or facing some problem that they need help with. When we as Christian women depend on the Holy Spirit, He will allow us to see beyond what our men are saying and doing, and reveal to us what their real needs are.

As Christian women, we can fight in the Spirit for our husbands, brothers, sons, neighbors and friends. Someone coined a phrase, "More things are changed by prayer, than this world dreams of." We do not have to despair when we see our men under the attack of the enemy, because we have the power to go into the spiritual realm and pray for the power of God to work in their lives. We must increase our prayers

Women Standing With Their Men

for our husbands to become the leaders God intended them to be. Too many times Satan causes us to get frustrated with our men instead of laboring in prayer for them. This happens when we take our focus off of God's ability, and we become overwhelmed by what we see in the natural.

When we see our mates going through difficulties, or in times of weakness, we must take them before the Lord in prayer and leave the situation in God's capable hands. We must seek God's wisdom about what to say and the right timing. Sometimes he will have us say nothing. Often Satan encourages us to talk more, when we should be praying more. I have found in my own experiences that when I truly give things to God, I have to do very little talking and explaining things. I just sit back and watch God work things out. When the Lord does instruct me to speak, I only say what He tells me to say. Words are powerful, they can heal or destroy. That's why the Scriptures admonish us to be swift to hear and slow to speak.

Christ told us to pick up our cross daily and deny ourselves. Deborah was a woman who sought the Lord for guidance, because she knew she was incapable of handling the difficulties and decisions she was faced with in her position as wife, spiritual leader and counselor. If we put our total trust in God and pray without ceasing, we will begin to see the ratio of men in our churches begin to increase dramatically.

I had a godly, praying mother who when her three sons were all addicted to cocaine, continued to pray until God set them all free, and saved them. My sisters and I were also praying for my brothers. My mother had the help of her daughters and

The Power In A Godly Woman

many other godly women in our church who believed God could do anything. Prayers went up for my brothers for over five years. During that time, one of them began living on the streets and sleeping in a car before he gave his life to Christ. Another brother lost his job and family, causing his four children to suffer. But we praying women did not allow these circumstances to discourage us. We were determined to continue praying until God delivered them. My mother also prayed for my father to be saved until she died. He died three years after my mom. But one year before he passed, Daddy accepted Christ in his life. Even though Momma was gone to be with the Lord and did not see my father turn his life over to God, her prayers were still working.

Sometimes when we pray God moves instantly, but many times we have to persevere and keep the faith, until our change comes. There are thousands of men and boys addicted to drugs and alcohol whose wives, mothers and sisters are praying for them. Some have grown weary and feel like giving up. But I encourage you to hold on and trust in God, because prayer does change things, and people. The Bible tells us, "The effectual fervent prayer of a righteous man availeth much" (James 5:16b KJV).

In our family, Satan didn't have a chance against all of that prayer power. We saw that cocaine is no match for God's power. Jesus died and made all of this power available to us, but it's up to us to use it.

Women Standing With Their Men

WORD POWER

We do not have to resort to this world's limited wisdom, but we should be directed by God's awesome Word. The Bible reveals to us the mind of God about everything. Hebrews 4:12 (KJV) tells us, "For the word of God is quick, and powerful, and sharper than any two edged sword, piercing even to the dividing asunder of soul and spirit, and of the joints and marrow, and is a discerner of the thoughts and intents of the heart." When I began to stand on what God's Word says and use it as a weapon to fight Satan's lies, tricks and deception, I began to walk in victory every day! Some of us are hitting and missing when it comes to winning spiritual battles, because we keep using fleshly weapons hoping to get spiritual results. We must fight spirit with spirit. Satan does not want us to realize who we are in Christ, so he keeps us distracted with people. I remember God getting my attention one day to let me know that I was spending too much time focusing on what people were saying or doing, instead of consistently viewing life through His eyes. Too often, people are ruled by their emotions, because they have so many areas where they have been wounded. Unfortunately, it blinds them spiritually.

Whenever we pray for our husbands, we should go to the Bible and get a passage of scripture that applies to their situation. Then we should begin praying that Word over them. God once spoke to me and said, "Joyce don't pray the problem, pray what My Word says about the problem." I have been doing so ever since, and it has made the difference in my level of faith and assurance when I pray. The Scriptures say that heaven and earth will pass away, but

His Word will stand forever. He also said that His Word will not return unto him void. Therefore, we can pray with confidence knowing that our prayers will be heard. Satan wants to destroy as many men as he can because he knows that the man carries the seed needed to produce life. In Genesis, the devil came to deceive the woman first, she then offered the fruit to the man. This is not to say that Adam was not responsible for his part in the fall, but just like then, Satan is still trying to use the woman to destroy the man whom God has placed as her head. Satan used Delilah to manipulate Sampson, and there are other examples of women throughout the Bible who influenced and manipulated men. Women, you are powerful beings. You can use that power for good or for the evil.

Principle #2

Meekness is not weakness; a godly woman possesses supernatural power.

CHRISTIAN WOMEN MUST FIND THEIR IDENTITY <u>IN CHRIST</u>

THREE

STANDING WITH OUR MEN

I interviewed the co-pastor of Power and Light Evangelistic Church, Geraldine Dozier. She and the senior pastor, Apostle Bennie Dozier, have been married for twenty-nine years. He has often said how grateful he is for how his wife has faithfully stood with him. Therefore, I knew she could give us some insight on this subject. Pastor Geri has been a pastor's wife for eighteen years; a position that comes with many challenges. I asked her to share some of her experiences with women and to explain how she managed to stand by her man for so long, despite many difficult situations she had to endure. I also asked Pastor Geri to do this interview because she was one of the few women whom I saw as a role model on how to stand by one's husband. She encouraged her husband and was his cheerleader.

I know there are many women, like myself, who had no idea how to build their mate up because of anger or frustration with men. That is why it is so important to pray for God to have a godly woman in your life who will not only give you sound wisdom, but one whom you have observed and can respect because she has lived it out in her own marriage. Pastor Geri said she struggled with low self-esteem and a spirit of fear for many years. After her husband accepted the call to be a pastor it magnified those problems in her life. She says she remembers crying out to the Lord many times, feeling overwhelmed and unable to accept a role she felt she was un-equipped to fill. Like many pastors' wives she knew her husband's role as a pastor would thrust her into the public eye. This was truly a frightening thought to her and she wanted no part of it. Pastor Geri felt a strong reluctance to accepting the inevitable intrusion into her life, marriage and home. She said she was well aware of the demands that would be placed upon her and her husband. She knew in order to be a blessing to him, and to the church, she would have to submit herself to the ministry to which they were called, without constantly murmuring and complaining. There were two things that made her determined to fight the fear and discomfort she was experiencing. First, it was her commitment to Christ, and secondly, her tremendous love for her husband and the desire to be the supporter he so desperately needed her to be.

There are many wives of pastors who are unhappy, and some are even miserable. Many are bitter and resentful because their husbands have neglected them by giving all of their time and attention to their pastoral duties, and their congregations. As a result, these women find it difficult, if not impossible, to give their husbands the support they want and need. Unfortunately, some pastors' wives have experienced many years of hurt, pain and frustration, because

Standing With Our Men

their husbands were unfaithful, unloving and inattentive. Some pastors treat their members better than they do their wives. Some women feel as if they are living with Dr. Jekel and Mr. Hyde; their husband is nice and sweet at church, but mean and unkind when he gets home. Often they feel they have no choice but to "go along" in order to save their marriages.

This was not the case with Pastor Geri, because she has a man who loves God, and loved his wife and children at home and at church. Her issues were personal insecurities and a lack of confidence in herself that she had to overcome. Pastor Geri said she turned to God and began to seek Him like never before. She knew that no matter how much she wanted to stand by her husband, if she did not get delivered from low self-esteem and the fear that was gripping her, she would be helpless to her mate. So, as Pastor Geri continued to pray, fast and study the Bible she began to discover her true identity as a Christian woman. She began to see herself as God saw her, a new creature in Christ Jesus. Geri decided to stand on what the Word of God said about every area of her life. She stood on the scripture that tells us, "For God hath not given us the spirit of fear; but of power, and of love, and of a sound mind." (2 Timothy 1:7 KJV)

After realizing her identity in Christ and seeing herself as more than a conqueror, through Christ, and knowing that God has not given her a spirit of timidity, her attitude about herself began to gradually turn around. She is now a strong, confident woman of God. Pastor Geri's advice to women who want to walk pleasing before the Lord, as they walk in God's divine plan for themselves, is that they must first find

Women Standing With Their Men

their identity in Christ. Women who are struggling with low self-esteem, fear, painful memories, and such, will find it difficult to be supportive of their mates. They are usually too focused on what they can do to fill the void in their own lives. Wounded people are very sensitive emotionally, and will react negatively to anything that resembles pain or rejection. Pastor Geri says that in order for a Christian woman to feel confident in her position in Christ, she must first establish an intimate relationship with God. This can only be done through prayer, fasting, reading, studying, obeying and applying God's Word to one's life. When wives take these steps and seek knowledge from God about every problem, or situation, in their lives, they will begin to address them from God's perspective, instead of reacting to their emotions. Subsequently, God will begin to show them how to relate to their husbands, and will give them wisdom on how to help them. This wisdom is necessary whether your mate is a Christian or not. 1 Corinthians 7:13-14

    Christian wives need the Holy Spirit to give them power and direction in standing with their husbands. Whenever you make a decision to do anything God's way, you must be prepared for opposition from the enemy. But if you follow the suggestions I have given you, you will be able to stand against any attack that comes your way.

Principle #3

Having an intimate relationship with Christ equips wives with strength and wisdom to stand with their husbands despite the difficulties.

MEN ARE WOUNDED TOO BUT MEN DON'T TELL

FOUR

UNDERSTANDING OUR MEN

Many wives struggle with standing by their husbands because they simply don't understand what makes them tick. The information that I will share in this chapter will help shed light on why men sometimes respond as they do.

A man can be wounded at any time during his life, but the injuries he experiences during childhood are the ones that have the most lasting impact, and the most far-reaching consequences. They may have wounds from physical or verbal battering, from sexual abuse, or from the absence of any genuine closeness with their father or mother. These are the wounds from the hundreds, perhaps thousands of times a little boy's heart ached for real love, and love was not there.

What's tragic is that not only has the child has been victimized by the misuse of parental power and authority, but this hurt little boy then conceals his feelings, his needs and his spirit. This profoundly injured little boy remains deep inside as he becomes a man.

Denying woundedness has sadly become the norm for manhood. This is the result of childhood-training from the family and, more broadly, from the culture that has given all of us—men and women—a very distorted notion of what manhood is all about. From this training, men have learned a certain code of behavior that causes them to hide away their natural expressiveness and, instead, come up with a way of acting "normal." Life becomes a game of 'let's pretend' wherein men continually try to get other people to buy their image but hide from most, perhaps even all, their true self. Most men you meet are trying to sell their image, whether they are aware of it or not.

For the majority of men, pretending started very early. The image, or role, they assumed was shaped from childhood, but was refined as they grew into manhood. They may have taken on the role of the perfectionist, the caretaker, the superhero, the invisible one, the macho man, the rebel, the nice guy, or any combination of these.

To cover their woundedness and depression, and cope with the underlying feelings that get harder to suppress as they get older, they may find themselves abusing alcohol, food, work, television, sex or something similar to ease their pain. It may develop that they are using either the substance, such as alcohol, or the activity, such as work, addictively, as a way of escaping from feelings that they don't know how to deal with. At the same time, whatever is used addictively will allow them to feel something.

For example, alcohol numbs the sensations while at the same time it releases inhibitions. Often, someone who would otherwise hold his feelings in, may be able to cry or laugh much more easily after one or two drinks. Sex, when used in an addictive way, can provide stimulation and release, yet

Understanding Our Men

at the same time may serve to cover and avoid other feelings, such as fear or sadness. Work when performed addictively can be an activity that lets men feel good about themselves because they are being productive and achieving, while concurrently helping them avoid intimacy or any personal dealings with other people.

I never remember my father saying the words I love you to me when I was growing up. I remember my father being a provider, but he didn't spend a lot of time with his twelve children. I later found out that he had started working and had taken care of himself since the age of twelve. He also had not received the attention and nurturing he needed as a little boy. Therefore, he was doing the best he could with what he knew. I was angry with my father for many years because it looked as if he did whatever he wanted to do, running around, going out drinking and coming in drunk. But on the other hand, my mother seemed to just sit around the house, have babies and wait on him.

I grew up determined I wasn't going to be like my mother and let some man do what he wanted to do and I do as he said do. I wasn't going to let some man put demands on me and be insensitive to my needs. That kind of attitude caused me a lot of problems in life, because it resulted in my being angry with all authority figures who seemed inconsistent in what they said versus what they did. I thank God I have been healed and delivered. The understanding I've gained about men has changed how I perceive those whom I felt were not being what God called them to be. I now have God's perspective, and it has set me free.

I know there are a lot of women, in the world, who are

angry like I was, but I want to inform you that Jesus is the key to your healing and freedom.

The Bible says it is very important that we seek understanding regarding the problems or confusing situations we find ourselves faced with. Even when things don't change immediately, we should seek to gain an understanding from God's eyes. Whenever I view things from God's perspective, it gives me the strength to cope with the circumstances and maintain my peace of mind until my change comes.

Principle #4

Men and women respond differently when they are wounded.

THE LORD GOD SAID
I WILL MAKE HIM A HELPER

FIVE

A HELPER

Let's look at what God spoke when He decided to create woman. "And the LORD God said, It is not good that the man should be alone; I will make him an help meet for him" (Gen. 2:18 KJV). God's original plan was for man and woman to work together in having dominion here on earth.

The problems between men and women began when sin entered the picture. When Adam and Eve sinned in the Garden of Eden by partaking of the fruit from the forbidden tree, it changed their relationship with God and with each other. The original state of purity in their fellowship with God and each other was destroyed. Whenever we listen to Satan's lies and deception, things get off track and we get out of God's divine will.

**MEN AND WOMEN
WORKING TOGETHER IN MINISTRY**

My husband is the senior pastor in our church, and

he takes a strong stand for God as a man and the head of our home. My position as co-pastor doesn't conflict with his role as my spiritual head because he knows he is God's delegated authority. He also recognizes that God is his head and that he is under God's authority. Unfortunately, we have women fighting against men, and men fighting against women. We have male ministers fighting against female ministers, in an unending cycle, it seems. It is for this reason, it is important that we look at the Bible's account of how God used men and women to carry out His purposes. When we operate from the Biblical perspective, it will eliminate the spirit of strife operating in many churches.

Women ministers have no need to feel pressured to prove that God uses women in ministry. In the Bible, there are many examples of how God used them in doing His will. When women do what God tells them, and don't waste time operating in bitterness and anger towards men who do not accept them, they can direct their energy towards fighting Satan, who is the real enemy. One of Satan's most effective strategies is to divide and conquer; he knows that division brings about weakness, and ultimately, destruction in any home or institution.

Even though I function in the office of co-pastor, in our church, my first ministry is to my husband. God let me know that my anointing is based on my obedience to Him and my submission to my husband. I have learned the power of submitting to my husband, whether I agree or not. As long as he does not ask me to do something sinful, then I must obey him in everything else. Submission doesn't mean I am not allowed to express my opinions. If I feel God is giving

A Helper

me something to share with my husband, I do so with the understanding that God is holding him accountable for the outcome, if he makes the wrong decision. Therefore, it is my responsibility to pray for my husband to have God's wisdom and obey the Lord's will in every matter. It is just as important when I share my thoughts with him, that it's done with respect for his position as my head. I also had to learn to wait and pray for God's timing to discuss certain matters, and not be opinionated when doing so. When my husband disagrees or feels God is saying something different, it is my responsibility to take it to the Lord and let God speak to him.

Anger and Frustration

I meet lots of angry and frustrated women who have been so wounded and disappointed, by the men in their lives, that they find it difficult to pray for their mates. If a woman does not get healing from the bitterness and resentment that is pent up inside, because of hurts, it will cause her to be guarded in her relationship with her husband. She will be reacting out of her pain unconsciously. It will also hinder her prayers for her mate.

Often, women find they are feeling depressed and angry, but can't seem to put their finger on where it's stemming from. I remember a situation where I felt I was handling a particular matter well, but when I was tested by situations that arose, it was clear I was still struggling with it. The reason I was unable to be objective was because I had grown weary of the situation and wanted it to be resolved. I felt I had some simple solutions that could fix the problem if only my husband was able to see them too.

When a person is faced with problems where they are feeling mentally and emotionally stressed for prolonged periods of time, it impacts them in a way they sometimes are unable to recognize. One of the reasons this happens in relationships is people usually do everything they can to avoid confrontations. Men are especially known for avoiding the discussion of problems, because they often feel they are no match for a woman when it comes to arguments. Most women are better at expressing their feelings in words than men.

It is crucial that couples learn to communicate effectively with each other so they do not harbor bitterness and resentment. When they don't get rid of these negative emotions it begins to erode their relationship without them even being aware of it. Sometimes couples don't realize their marriage has deteriorated until it is too late. When a root of bitterness goes unchecked it will eventually grow into a tall tree full of branches and leaves full of pain. And sometimes it becomes almost impossible to up root. There are instances where problems have festered so long, that one or both spouses are unwilling to put in the time and effort it will take to bring about healing so, unfortunately, they choose to go their separate ways.

The statistics indicate that the divorce rate in the church is just as high as it is with unsaved couples. Believers have an advantage in every area of life including marriage, because God has already given us the answers to life in His Word. If Christian couples are going to enjoy the benefits of having the Holy Spirit in their marriages, they must be willing to obey

A Helper

God's instructions about the husband's and wife's assigned responsibilities in the relationship. Whenever we follow the Lord's plan, we will have marriages made in heaven.

As women, we should always be praying for God's wisdom, about ways to be a helper to our husbands. We should not live our lives based on what others are doing; we should always seek God's master plan for your own marriage. Too often, we get the opinions of others rather than God's.

Accept Him Where He Is

Some women are unaware that the reason their frustration level with their husband exists is because they have unrealistic expectations. One of the greatest lessons I have had to learn, as a wife, is to appreciate my husband where he is, even though I may be praying for God to help him grow in a particular area. I know we want our husbands to give us the same consideration, because none of us is perfect. It is amazing how we expect others to look beyond our faults and see our needs, but too often we do not return the favor. We have a tendency to have preconceived notions about what is acceptable to us, and become irritated when others don't measure up.

I encourage wives to get to know your husband's strengths and weaknesses. Pray that God will help you not to focus on his weaknesses all the time. When a wife keeps looking at her husband's shortcomings it will cause her to become frustrated. If a wife will continue to pray for her husband in areas that she sees a need for change, or growth, instead of constantly complaining about them, she will experience the peace of God in her relationship with him.

I have seen so many couples living together, yet they are miserable. Often, the husband or wife talk about dreading the time they have to be in the presence of their spouse. There are some couples who communicate on an as needed basis. Some mates even use silence as a weapon to hurt their mate or as a way of protecting themselves from further pain. If there are children in the home, they have to live in this toxic environment.

His Responsibility

Jesus is a perfect example of what the husband's attitude should be towards his wife. Just as Christ gave himself for the church, men carry a great responsibility in being the head. The Scriptures tell them they must love their wives as Christ loved the church.

The idea of man being the head over the woman originated with God.

Unto the woman he said, I will greatly multiply thy sorrow and thy conception; in sorrow thou shalt bring forth children; and thy desire shall be to thy husband, and he shall rule over thee.
(Genesis 3:16 KJV)

But I would have you know, that the head of every man is Christ; and the head of the woman is the man...
(1 Corinthians 11:3a KJV)

A Helper

It doesn't matter how liberated a woman is, or thinks she is, she is still not the head when it comes to the man. What does God mean when He tells the man that he is head over the woman? God means the man is to be the leader in his home. What is a leader? A leader is an influencer, one who guides and directs either the right way or the wrong way. The leader is also the one who is held responsible when things don't turn out right. His failure sets a poor example for those he is leading. Being the head, as God sees it, doesn't mean you get to boss people around; it means that the final responsibility rests on you. When I finally got that revelation of headship, I was more than happy to submit to my husband, and began to pray that he hears from God about every decision made. If we both want to do what is pleasing in God's sight, we realize we must seek the Lord's will in every matter. As Jesus so often said while here on earth, "I came not to do my will, but my Father's will." Jesus was totally submitted to His Father, and we need to follow His example.

My husband has often expressed his appreciation for how much I have helped him through the love and support I give him. I found the saying, "Behind every good man, is a good woman" to be very true. Whoever coined that phrase understood well the power of two individuals working together. Men and women both have strong points, and they should balance one another because God designed it that way. Too often, we are so focused on our spouse's shortcomings that we miss all the positive traits he has. Occasionally, I take time to itemize my husband's strong points, and my respect and appreciation for him increases, and it reminds me of how many wonderful qualities he possesses.

The Difference In Male and Female Thinking

Dr. Myles Monroe in his book *Understanding the Purpose and Power of Men*, describes the differences in males and females this way.

God created men and women with perfectly complementary designs. The male is perfect for the female, and the female is perfect for the male. It is when men and women expect each other to think, react, and behave in the same ways—that is, when they don't know or appreciate their God-given differences—that they experience conflict.

Yet when they understand and value each other's purposes, they can have rewarding relationships, and they can blend their unique designs harmoniously for God's glory.

Men and women usually see things differently because their brains don't operate the same. I have consulted with my husband on many occasions and he will shed light in one or more areas that I had never considered. We do not agree in every matter, but we have learned to listen and respect one another's opinions, and pray about the differences. Often women respond in the way they do because they were never taught the differences; therefore, the wife keeps expecting her

A Helper

husband to see things the way she does. I remember feeling a level of relief once I had gained more understanding of how men think and respond. I, like many other wives, thought there was something uniquely wrong with men and was confused about how I might help my husband. Many couples marry without getting premarital counseling. Therefore, women marry having limited knowledge and understanding about what the role of the wife is. Add to that fact that often she has not been exposed to enough positive marriage role models, and in some cases none, therefore, she is ill equipped to stand with her husband and support him through the difficult times. Even though she may want to function in her role as helper, her limited understanding as to what her role should be hinders her from doing so. This book was written to give wives the information and principles needed to fulfill their desire to be helpers, instead of hindrances, to their husbands.

Principle #5

Helping our men is a responsibility assigned to women by God.

A MAN'S HOME
IS HIS PALACE

SIX

A SPIRIT-FILLED HOME

There is a saying that I heard many times while growing up, "A man's home is his castle." This statement was usually made to emphasize the importance of a man having a place where he could escape and have peace of mind. Home was to be a place where he felt respected and where he was king. Today, many women would say that this slogan is archaic because it does not fit with the liberal women's philosophy. I often tell women I do everything I can to make my husband feel like a king, because that automatically makes me the queen! I look for ways to make my husband as comfortable as I can when he is home. At one time I was a working woman, pastor and business woman, and I began to make excuses about why things weren't done in my home. I felt due to my extremely busy schedule my husband should be understanding when I didn't wash dishes, or keep my house as tidy as we were used to. But God let me know that my first ministry was to my husband, and everything else comes after that. I found that when I listened and obeyed God's counsel our home and relationship became more and more peaceful, and loving. It caused Les and I to grow closer than ever.

I believe most men still view their home as their palace. When they come home to a place where they can relax from the stresses of their day, and feel loved, appreciated and supported it makes all the difference in the world. Because so many women work outside of the home, and often on different shifts from their husbands, the nurturing that our men need is often neglected. Women who work are often stressed out themselves from getting the children to childcare and school, working all day in stressful environments, and having to come home to prepare dinner. That makes it difficult to be focused on encouraging and comforting your mate, when you need someone to comfort you. But it does not negate the need for husbands and wives to be supportive of and sensitive to each other.

Christians must see our homes as more than a place to escape from the world. Instead, we should think of them as the central headquarters for planning our strategy for kingdom-building. Our homes should be the place where we get together to plan for battle against our enemy. Christian homes should also be models for the world to see love, harmony and wholeness. The unsaved should desire to emulate the peace, unity, understanding and respect they see in Christian marriages. That is not to say believers don't have problems in their marriages, but the way they handle these issues should be totally different from the world.

I have heard many adults and even young people who say they will never marry because of the poor examples they saw in their parents or other family members' relationships. We are living in a generation that believes living together is

A Spirit-Filled Home

normal. Some have told me they don't feel that they need a piece of paper (marriage license) to prove anything. They also expressed that if a relationship doesn't work out it is easier to walk away if they are not married.

In many homes, men are not carrying out their God-given responsibilities as leaders in their domain. Some aren't even aware of what their roles are because they have never been taught, or did not have proper role models when they were growing up. Some men believe being the head of their home means being the boss over their wife and children, and being served by them, instead of being a servant to them as Jesus did. Thus, they are not following the example of how Jesus treats His bride, the church. Husbands are to lay down their lives for their wives and children, and they have been given the responsibility, by God, to be the spiritual leaders in their homes.

There are many instances where wives are unwilling, for a variety of reasons, to submit to their husbands and to encourage them in their God-given role as head. I struggled with submitting, also, because I was such an independent person. As a result of personal situations and negative relationships with men, in my life, I was very rebellious when it came to men. Through prayer and spiritual growth, I have been delivered in this area, and I became knowledgeable as it relates to God's delegated authority.

Many women say they want their husbands to be the leader in their family, but for various reasons the man abdicates his responsibility. Some men prefer to let their wives handle most of the stressful situations that arise in families. For example, when it comes to dealing with paying bills, problems with the children, etc., many husbands and fathers avoid involvement. They feel their primary responsibility is to provide financially for the family.

Usually, when this happens, most women simply do what they feel they have to do in order to keep things going. Thus, women have a lot of added stress that they should not have to endure. There are some situations that may require immediate attention, but whenever possible, women need to encourage their husbands to get involved, even if it is no more than asking their opinion about a matter. Many women are experiencing excessive mental and emotional stress because they don't allow or encourage their husbands to carry their part of the load.

When husbands and wives work through their problems together, it helps to build a healthy relationship. When couples help bear one another's burdens, it brings them closer together, and the bond between them is strengthened. If the wife maintains a positive attitude and prays for her husband, the Holy Spirit will give her the wisdom on how to discuss family problems and situations. No matter how resistant your husband may be, if you pray and keep the faith, God can touch his heart. The key is standing by your husband while you wait on God to bring change in situations. It is crucial that we obey the Word of God by walking by faith and not by sight.

The New Testament gives a wonderful account of a spirit-filled couple working together for the Lord. Aquilla and Priscilla worked diligently together, serving the apostle Paul in their home and even traveling from place to place with him. I'm sure every day wasn't perfect, but they had one main goal,

A Spirit-Filled Home

and that was to spread the gospel wherever they went.

One of the most beautiful things you can witness is when a husband and wife join forces to work together. Satan doesn't have a chance against two Spirit-filled, Spirit-led, committed people.

GODLY CONVERSATION

There are many Christian women who are married to unsaved or carnal-minded men. Carnal-minded men are men who profess to be Christians, who go to church on Sunday, but live the opposite outside of the church. In both cases, it is unlikely these men will be the spiritual heads of their households, because they are not being directed by the Holy Spirit. Many wives who are Spirit-filled and living for God, and want to live pleasing before the Lord, feel the negative pull of their ungodly mates. Unfortunately, in many of these situations the wife is not following what the Word of God says to her.

Likewise, ye wives, be in subjection to your own husbands; that, if any obey not the word, they also may without the word be won by the conversation of the wives; While they behold your chaste conversation coupled with fear. Whose adorning let it not be that outward adorning of plaiting the hair, and of wearing of gold, or of putting on of apparel; But let it be the hidden man of the heart, in that which is not corruptible, even the ornament of a meek and quiet spirit, which is in the sight of God of great price. (1 Peter 3:1-4 KJV).

Women Standing With Their Men

The term unbelieving refers to the unsaved husband, but it can also be used to describe men who are in the church but are not living according to God's Word. Sometimes there are situations where a husband is saved, but there are many, such as the aforementioned areas, where he needs to grow. When women obey the Scriptures they will aid in their husband's spiritual growth by their godly example. Your life may be the only Bible he is reading right now. It is important that Christian women be patient and be willing to pray for their husbands no matter how long it takes. I am not saying that a woman who is being physically or verbally abused remain in an unhealthy situation. This, meanwhile, does not mean she has to divorce her husband, but she should remove herself from a violent or life-threatening situation as she continues to pray for God's will about the marriage.

When Christian women allow the Holy Spirit to guide them as to how to be the kind of wife God wants them to be, they will see the power of God in their homes. Their relationships will be enhanced, and their children will see healthy role models which will have a positive affect on them when they are ready to start their families. It will also cause the divorce rate among Christian couples to drop.

I know of many couples who have been married for years but they don't have peace in their homes. Sometimes the husband or the wife, or both of them, stay busy just to avoid one another. Many stay together until their children leave home and then divorce, because they did not address their issues God's way. Instead, they allowed the animosity to build up between them. So they tolerate each other until what they deem is a convenient time to dissolve the relationship. It is sad, but true, that you have untold thousands of Christian couples who are living together, yet are miserable. Many times they stay together because they believe it is the Christian thing to do, but don't believe that things can get any better. I have met pastors, ministers, deacons, and the list goes on, who are sitting in churches every Sunday, but are miserable at home. This is why the door is open for so much infidelity in the church. Satan capitalizes on all the hurt and pain and unhappiness between couples, in the church, by putting someone in their path who seems to have all the characteristics that are missing in their mate. He orchestrates what often seems to be an innocent situation to get the two together, and the rest is history. The Bible says we must know the devil's devices.

Principle #6

A Christian home should be filled with the presence of God.

THE HOLY SPIRIT GIVES POWER TO MEN AND WOMEN

SEVEN

BALANCED POWER

As women of God, we have an important role that was given to us by the Creator. We know that our men could not make it without us, because God created us to 'HELP' them. We are first of all to help them at home, then in our neighborhoods, our communities and of course the church. When we look inside church doors throughout America, unfortunately, congregations are predominately comprised of women and children. Women have persevered throughout the centuries, and like Deborah, have stood no matter what came their way. God placed the strength in women they needed for childbearing and marriage. In both cases they come with pain and joy.

Unto the woman he said, I will greatly multiply thy sorrow and thy conception; in sorrow thou shalt bring forth children; and thy desire shall be to thy husband, and he shall rule over thee. (Genesis 3:16 KJV)

It doesn't matter how strong we are ladies, because of Eve's sin in the garden, we have been given a mandate by God, and he said our husbands are to rule over us. This is called delegated authority.

But I would have you know, that the head of every man is Christ; and the head of the woman is the man...
(1 Corinthians 11:3a KJV).

WHAT IS DELEGATED AUTHORITY

For many years I had a problem with submitting to authority figures, especially males, as I've mentioned earlier. My feeling was that I should only obey those in authority when I felt their behavior or decisions were right. I had no knowledge about 'delegated authority.' Therefore, I responded to those in authority by invariably being rebellious. This behavior affected my response to authority figures in my home, on my job and in the church. But God, in his mercy allowed me to gain knowledge about delegated authority, when I began to seek Him on why I kept having confrontations with anyone who was in charge. I was drawing closer to God, and I asked Him to reveal to me whatever was hindering my relationship with Him.

I was given a book written by Watchman Nee called *Spiritual Authority*. The following are excerpts from this book that God used to educate me on delegated authority.

God is the source of all authorities in the universe. Now since all governing authorities are instituted by Him, then all authorities are delegated by Him and represent His authority. God Himself has established this system of authority in order to manifest Himself.

Balanced Power

Those who are set up by God are to exercise authority for Him. Since all governing authorities are ordained and instituted by God, they are meant to be obeyed. If we indeed learn how to obey God, we would then have no trouble recognizing on whom God's authority rests. But if we know only God's direct authority, we may possibly violate more than half of His authority.

As to earthly authorities, Paul not only exhorts positively towards subjection but also warns negatively against resistance. He who resists the authorities resists God's own command; he who rejects God's delegated authorities rejects God's own authority. He who resists authority resists God, and those who resist will incur judgment. There is no possibility of rebellion without judgment. The consequence of resisting authority is death. Man has no choice in the matter of authority.

After having read Watchman Nee's book, I clearly understood God's expectations as it related to obeying authority. God let me know that it was not my place to straighten an authority out, when I thought he was wrong, as I had done in so many instances. He told me my only job was to obey and pray for delegated authority, as long as they were not asking me to sin against Him. I began to do exactly what I was told and it changed my whole life. I was not irritated and angry all the time. I began to walk in the peace of God, and I'm still doing so today. God's way always gets you the best. Another thing

I came to realize is that even though a person is in authority they are accountable to someone too. The Bible says we will always reap what we sow, no matter what our position is. I am a person in several positions of authority, but because I am keenly aware of the sowing and reaping principle, I never use my position to mistreat or take advantage of anyone.

DELEGATED AUTHORITY IN THE HOME

God has set the husband as the delegated authority of Christ, with the wife representative of the church. It would be difficult for the wife to be subject to her husband if she did not see the delegated authority vested in Him by God. She needs to realize that the real issue is God's authority, not her husband's.

....Submitting yourselves one to another in the fear of God. Wives, submit yourselves unto your own husbands, as unto the Lord. For the husband is the head of the wife, even as Christ is the head of the church: and he is the saviour of the body. Therefore as the church is subject unto Christ, so let the wives be to their own husbands in every thing. (Ephesians 5:21-24 KJV)

Watchman Nee's book on spiritual authority helped me realize that submitting to delegated authority would not make me vulnerable or deprive me of my rights, as Satan constantly tried to convince me was the case. Instead, I discovered that submitting to authority puts one in a position of favor with God and it allows them to soar, like an eagle, in the spiritual realm.

Balanced Power

God spoke to me one day while in prayer, and gave me a perspective on submission that I had never heard or read about. What he revealed to me was, "Rebellion always produces cursing in any relationship, but conversely, submission always produces blessings." This revelation helped me to truly understand and appreciate the significance of submitting to my husband. This explains why so many Christian homes are in chaos and the peace of God does not abide there. Whenever we fail to operate our lives according to God's divine order stated in the Scriptures, "the head of every woman is man, and the head of every man is Christ," it opens the door for our enemy to come in and deprive us of God's blessings.

When I researched the word 'rebellion' I discovered there were numerous negative attitudes and behaviors associated with it. The Bible tells us that rebellion is as witchcraft, which is an indication of the seriousness of women operating in this spirit in relation to their husbands and men in relation to God. Whenever husbands and wives open the door to Satanic activity through rebellion it will ultimately affect their children and the environment in their home.

When wives operate in a spirit of submission, they will cause continuous blessings to flow in their marriage, children, and their home. This is why it is imperative that women avoid operating in rebellion with their husbands. The Bible says in Proverbs, living with a rebellious woman is vexation to a man's soul. Many rebellious women have destroyed their marriages and were unaware that the real problem stemmed from rebellion.

BALANCED POWER

Wives don't have to despair because Jesus Christ brought BALANCE through the Holy Spirit. When it comes to spiritual matters, there is no male and female in the Holy Spirit. We have the same spiritual power as men. But that does not eliminate God's divine order. The Scriptures tell us that God has no respect of persons.

For ye are all the children of God by faith in Christ Jesus. For as many of you as have been baptized into Christ have put on Christ. There is neither Jew nor Greek, there is neither bond nor free, there is neither male nor female: for ye are all one in Christ Jesus.
(Galatians 3:26-28 KJV)

The Bible tells us God did not limit His Holy Spirit to any one race or group of people. He said all who will believe on Jesus will receive the gift of His Holy Spirit. As women of God we are empowered to help build the kingdom of God. We cannot do it without the man, and neither can they do it without us. That's the way God designed things. Only God deserves the glory for whatever we accomplish, while we are here.

In print and electronic media, we see and hear many messages that downplay commitment in marriage, that promote lifestyles that are not in line with God's Word. That's why it is so important that Christian homes reflect God's viewpoint on marriage and the family. The media is being used to promote division, instead of unity, between the sexes. The reason Satan is using this strategy is because he knows if he

Balanced Power

succeeds with his divide and conquer schemes, it will affect our families and society as a whole. But most importantly, it will affect mankind's relationship with God, and our ability to build His kingdom, or way of doing things, here on earth.

Principle #7

The Holy Spirit does not operate based on gender; men and women have equal power in the spiritual realm.

HEALED PEOPLE BRING HEALING TO OTHERS

Eight

HURT PEOPLE, HURT PEOPLE

During the dating and engagement process, couples often don't take time to investigate one another's past to determine what kind of past hurts are being brought into the present relationship. Usually, people work hard to present their positive side in the beginning stages of a courtship. And even if one or both parties show they are hurting, it is often overlooked because they are afraid of losing the other person. Couples, also, are more sympathetic during the dating phase, and sometimes feel they are the answer to helping the other person with his or her problems. If people are not willing to take an honest look at the individual they are considering for a lifetime partner, they may regret that decision later.

Many times, people who are in love with a person who is clearly struggling with bitterness and anger from past hurts, will make the statement, "I feel God has put me in their life to help them." But what they are really saying is, "I'm going to fix them, and everything will be fine once we get married." Of course we all know that is the furthest thing from the truth. Usually, their spouse is the last person they will listen to. Oftentimes, the spouse gets blamed for or receives the backlash from those past hurts.

When a couple is in the courtship phase, of their

relationship, they should use that time to find out everything they can about the other person's childhood and family history; especially what the person's relationship was with their mother and father when they were growing up and what it is today. They should also find out what the medical and mental history is for the person they are dating, as well as their family's medical and mental history.

    This is so important for many reasons, but especially because it will affect any children coming into the marriage. It is amazing how many people marry someone they hardly know. People often end up falling in love with a person based on who they thought that person was, and later discover their mate was not honest with them. When you meet someone who is unwilling to discuss their past in detail with you, it is usually an indication they have something to hide, or they have been wounded so badly they find it too painful to talk about it. When this happens, it is wise to push for more details, because you could be dealing with a very angry and bitter person, or someone who has been traumatized in their childhood and has not been able to get past the pain of it. In either situation, it will affect your relationship and ultimately your marriage. It is always best to find out sooner rather than later, and work through things before you go into covenant with a person. Unfortunately, these are some of the reasons why the divorce rate is alarmingly high among believers.

    I was told about a woman who dated a man for over a year, and during this time she said he was a perfect gentleman. He would take her out to dinner and buy her flowers and gifts and showed her only gentleness and kindness. But after she married him, she said he became a

Hurt People, Hurt People

completely different person. He was mean, verbally and physically abusive, jealous and controlling. She said she cried almost every day, because he had betrayed her while they were dating. When I heard this story, I felt sad for her, but I also questioned if she really never had any signs of his true or other personality, or was she so caught up in his kind gestures that she ignored the warning signs. This could easily happen if she is a woman who is desperate for love and affection. When a woman has grown up in an environment where she did not receive love and support it's easy to be swept off her feet by someone who is extremely nice to her.

Then there are instances where you have a man who is a very giving individual, and he meets a woman who has been so wounded in a previous relationship that she is totally focused on getting her own needs met. When this occurs, the man will ultimately end up feeling frustrated and used. He will also become angry and bitter because the woman he has married is not able to meet his needs because she is too consumed with nursing her own pain. This is another reason why it is so important to take time to really get to know the person you plan to marry.

When you are married to a person who is deeply wounded, it is unrealistic to expect that person to be able to meet your needs until they have been healed themselves. When someone is struggling with past hurts, they often become defensive, protective and see themselves as a victim. They will go to great lengths to protect themselves from any further violation, or perceived pain. Living with an individual like this takes prayer and wisdom as to how you can keep peace in your home, while you allow them to go through the healing process. It is not your role to rescue them or to carry the weight of what has happened to them. It is difficult to watch someone you love be miserable every day, but you cannot allow it to make your life unbearable.

A woman's nurturing instincts usually causes her to react by trying to get her husband to talk to her so she can help him. Unfortunately, men often are unwilling to open up and share what is on their hearts because they feel this makes them vulnerable. They also don't want to appear as if they are weak in front of their wives. When your husband is unwilling to discuss a matter with you, it sometimes feels like he is being secretive or rejecting you. Some women continue to push for information which only exasperates the situation, and often leads to quarrelling and being angry with one another.

When women who are in relationships with hurting men begin to seek God's wisdom through prayer, fasting, and being led by the Holy Spirit, they will see the power of God bring healing to their husbands. There are places where we hurt that only God can touch and heal. Believers have an advantage in having the Holy Spirit to guide us as we seek direction from Him. Jesus said that he was sending back the Spirit, who would be our counselor and would lead and guide us into all truth. The Holy Spirit is able to give us discernment far beyond what we see on the surface. If wives would utilize the wisdom that is available to us, we would less often rack our brains trying to figure out what to do for our husbands. All you have to do is pray and ask the Holy Spirit to reveal to you how to be a help instead of a hindrance to your husband's healing process.

Principle #8

Wounded people will continue to wound others, until their own wounds are healed.

ARE YOU HEALED?

Nine

ARE YOUR WOUNDS HEALED?

When a wife is struggling with her own unresolved issues, she will be limited in her ability to help her husband. In a marriage where the husband and wife are both nursing past wounds, their relationship will be difficult, at best. Women are very good at putting their own circumstances on the back burner, while they focus on what their husband is going through. But what wives don't realize is that their pain is festering like a sore that has gone unattended. Before she becomes too consumed with helping her husband, she has to make sure she is praying about her own issues. That doesn't mean she is being selfish, but until she receives healing, for herself, she will be limited in her ability to help her spouse. It is difficult to rescue someone who is drowning, when you are going under yourself. The Bible tells us to comfort others, with the comfort we have received.

There are wives who become so focused on their own pain that they are unable to see what their husbands are struggling with. This is especially true when a wife was

Women Standing With Their Men

hurt in a previous relationship and has not healed from it. Sometimes, there is an issue of still having spiritual soul ties to another person. There are situations where a wife was in a mentally or physically abusive relationship and she never received counseling. There are wives who have been sexually abused as children and never received counseling. In some instances, it was a close relative or her mother's boyfriend. When a woman brings this kind of unresolved pain into any relationship her husband will suffer the fallout. Some women are very angry and bitter most of the time and make their homes a very unpleasant place to live. They nag and complain, and are constantly critical, making for a miserable situation.

  The wife I just described will not be able to stand by her husband unless she is healed. No amount of money, gifts, or material things given to her by her husband can make up for the pain she lives with daily. Too often, she is looking to her husband to rescue her from her pain, but he doesn't have a clue where to begin. Husbands often become irritated and confused after they have tried everything they know, to do, to make their wife happy. Sometimes she cries and isolates herself. He doesn't know how to respond to the anger and rejection she doles out to him. This is a perfect breeding ground for Satan to come in and make matters worse because of the spirit of strife operating between them. When this happens and there are children in the home, they have to live in a residence where the atmosphere is cold and tense. Parents often forget how much their relationship with one another impacts the mental health of their children.

  We have a Heavenly Father who cares and is waiting

Are Your Wounds Healed?

for us to allow Him to bring healing in our lives. Often we become consumed with the circumstances of life and lose focus, however, on God. Women play a crucial role in the home, and if the wife is not healed, herself, she will be unable to remain sensitive to her husband and pray him into healing.

Wives must be honest about their own spiritual condition, and pray as they seek refuge and healing in the arms of God. It is important to periodically ask God to open our eyes to see things spiritually that the natural eye will miss. In the book of 1 Peter, God instructs Christian women to have a meek and quiet spirit. This is not possible when a woman is full of pain, hurt, bitterness and resentment. When we go to God with our hurts, He is able to heal us of whatever has happened to us. He can do what appears to be impossible for us.

There were several times in my own life where my heart was aching, and one time, in particular, when I felt like my heart was broken in a thousand pieces. This was not caused by my husband, but I knew that he would be affected by it if I did not receive healing. I asked God to heal me, and He healed my heart in a matter of seconds. Only Almighty God has the power to heal someone of that depth of pain. After God did that for me, I became even more sensitive to others who I saw hurting deeply. I can comfort them with the comfort that God allowed me to experience. This has happened to me on several occasions, and each time I experience God's awesome power, in this way, it increases my faith and trust in Him. It makes me want to praise Him like never before. There are situations that cause such a depth of pain that no human can help you. I know if my husband could have comforted me during those times he would have.

I have counseled many women who reach out to their husbands to be comforted, by them, and have walked away more hurt or frustrated than they were before they talked with them. There are times it may seem as if your husband is being insensitive, but he can only respond based on his level of understanding and spiritual maturity. It is important that we don't have unrealistic expectations of our mates. For example, if you know that your husband is spiritually immature, you should not expect him to respond to you as if he *is* mature. He can only give out what is in him.

Principle #9

It is difficult to comfort someone else while you are in pain.

ARE YOU EXPECTING THE ONE WHO CAUSED YOU PAIN TO HEAL YOU?

TEN

ARE YOU EXPECTING THE PERSON WHO HURT YOU TO HEAL YOU?

One of the most difficult situations a wife has to deal with in her marriage is to be hurt by her husband. This could be the result of a husband who is physically, verbally or emotionally abusive. When a wife is living with a man who is hurting, who either is unable to see it, or unsure how to handle his pain, she may be hurt by him over and over, again. That does not mean that he is doing it intentionally. And though he may not be aware of his behavior, it does not lessen how it affects the wife.

There are thousands upon thousands of wives who are suffering from pain inflicted on them by their husbands. But what is even worse, these women are looking to the men who hurt them to heal them. Some are confused as to how someone who tells them "I love you" in one breath, can continue to hurt them over and over again.

In their attempts to seek sympathy or comfort from

their husbands, many wives will try to explain to their spouses how they feel. Unfortunately, they often walk away even more wounded, because their husband cannot see what he is doing, because he is blinded by his own pain. So the cycle continues, and the marriage becomes more strained each day.

An example of someone whom I watched go through this cycle is a woman whose husband was abandoned by his mother as a child. Therefore, whatever his wife did was always suspect to him, and he was very insecure because he felt his wife would abandon him; in addition, he was a person who could not take criticism, or accept responsibility for anything that went wrong in the home. His wife tried for years to show him the error of his ways, but of course he wasn't going to accept it, because he couldn't see himself. She came to me once when she was at the end of her rope. She was ready to walk away from the marriage because she had had enough.

This wife also admitted that she had been hurt as a child, as well, and was unable to endure any more pain, herself. I took time to explain that her husband's attacks were not a result of him not loving her, nor were they intentional. I wanted to help her see that he was in too much pain from his childhood, and he needed her to be patient with him.

Most importantly, I told her not to expect her husband to feel sorry for the things he said and had done to her, because most of the time he wasn't aware of how he was impacting her. Therefore, more often than not, he would be unsympathetic when she made him aware of how she felt. I told her the first thing she needed to do was forgive her husband for everything he had ever done to her, because if she harbored unforgiveness and bitterness, it would hinder her prayers for their marriage. I

Are You Expecting The Person Who Hurt You To Heal You?

told her one way to do that was she needed to see her husband as part of her and not as her enemy. She needed to keep in her mind that when he was hurting it was like her hurting; and just like she would want him to look beyond her faults and see her needs, if the roles were reversed, she needed to do the same for him. It was also important that she asked God to forgive her for any wrong feelings she had held against him. I reminded her of what Jesus said: "If we won't forgive others, neither will [He] forgive us."

I also encouraged her to pray more and talk less to him. I advised her to only talk to her husband when the Holy Spirit told her to, and to only say what the Spirit was saying for that moment. This is important because too often when God does give a wife something to tell her husband, she wants to add a lot of things she has been waiting to tell him. This will always backfire, because your husband will only receive what God has prepared his heart to accept.

This woman decided one day she was going to fight for her marriage. She went on a fast for several days and prayed for God to deal with her heart first. She now understood that if her marriage was going to survive, she was the one who was going to have to stand in the gap for it. She also knew that she could not pray for her husband, as he needed her to, until she was honest about the bitterness and unforgiveness she had been struggling with herself. She also needed God to heal her of her wounds. She told me when she finished her fast that God had healed her, and He also gave her compassion for her husband. She said she made up her mind during that time that she was going to stand no matter how difficult things got. She knew that the enemy was going to fight her on this, and she had to have a made up mind in order to win the battle for her marriage. She was now looking to God to meet the needs her husband could not meet at that point. Her decision was to love her husband no matter how he treated her, because she knew God was going to deal with him. She also knew that God would protect her from him going too far. The reason many wives give up on praying for their husbands is because the devil tells them that their husband will make a fool out of them, or that she must stand up for herself. When a wife is trusting God, she doesn't need to worry because God will give her wisdom, and the Lord will protect her.

The saying 'hurt people, hurt people' is so true. A person can only give out of their heart what is there. So, for a wife to expect her husband to be sensitive, understanding and gentle towards her when he has been deeply wounded is unrealistic. Jesus said you can't get sweet water out of a bitter fountain. In order for a wife to stand by her husband under these circumstances, she cannot expect her spouse to heal the emotional wounds he inflicts on her. She must trust God to do that! This woman who was so bitter and angry, she had lost all of her joy and peace, but she was healed and restored by God. After God healed her, it was obvious because you could see it on her face.

Circumstances don't always change immediately when you are praying about a situation, but God will always give you peace in the midst of whatever you are going through. The Scriptures tell us not to walk by sight, but, instead, by faith. Christians have an advantage because of what Jesus made available to us. When Jesus died, the veil of the temple

Are You Expecting The Person Who Hurt You To Heal You?

was torn from top to bottom, giving us direct access to our Heavenly Father twenty-four hours a day, seven days a week. I am a witness that nobody can comfort you like God. He will wipe away your tears and turn your sorrow into gladness. He will make you strong when you feel weak. He can heal hurts that no human being can begin to take away.

God has given us our husbands to be there for us in many ways, but they are often limited, just as wives are, because they are human. The Bible says don't put your confidence in man, but put all your trust in the Lord. God will never let you down!

Principle #10

The person that hurts you can't help you heal if they aren't healed.

A WISE WOMAN
IS CONSTRUCTIVE

Eleven

A WISE WOMAN BUILDS HER HOUSE

When I was growing up, I heard wives say a lot of things that I now understand wasn't wise. I have heard older women tell young women, "always keep some money hidden from your husband for a rainy day." I am sure they were saying what they heard someone else say, but it definitely did not come from the Word of God. It is unfortunate that we don't have more Christian wives who are godly role models.

In order for a wife to be wise and build her house, she must make sure her view of what a wife should be lines up with God's Word. If Christian wives are going to build their house, they must ask God for His wisdom in every matter. Too often, Christian wives take their cues from women who do not profess to know Christ. These women could be from their family, unsaved acquaintances and some even follow what they see on television. If a person is not following God it will be unlikely they will be able to give you godly wisdom. This can also be true of women who attend church every Sunday, because, unfortunately, many Christian women don't pray and look to the Bible to get their wisdom from God. Therefore, you have women in the church giving other women worldly advice they were given or picked up along the way.

The woman described in Proverbs 31 is a good role model for wives.

**Who can find a virtuous woman? for her price is far above rubies. The heart of her husband doth safely trust in her, so that he shall have no need of spoil. She will do him good and not evil all the days of her life.
(Proverbs 31:10-12 KJV)**

**Strength and honour are her clothing; and she shall rejoice in time to come. She openeth her mouth with wisdom; and in her tongue is the law of kindness. She looketh well to the ways of her household, and eateth not the bread of idleness. Her children arise up, and call her blessed; her husband also, and he praiseth her.
(Proverbs 31:25-28 KJV)**

Virtuous and Capable

A virtuous woman is one who is highly moral and is a woman of excellence. She is also competent because she has the Holy Spirit who empowers her and gives her wisdom when making decisions about her family and home. Therefore, whatever she does will result in her house being built up instead of being torn down.

A Wise Woman Builds Her House

Trust

When a husband can trust his wife, it adds strength to his very being. He has confidence in her because he is assured that she does everything with his best interest at heart. My husband has often told me that I was the first woman he trusted to the degree he does. He says he knows I love the Lord, therefore, I will know how to love him as well. He also said I am the only woman he has ever trusted with his money. And that is because he trusts the God in me to lead me to do what is right and honest.

Helps, Not Hinders

God created wives to be a help to their husbands. When a wife operates in the wisdom of God, she will not hinder her husband by saying or doing things that will hold him back from being his best. She will be careful to speak words of encouragement. Too often, wives who have had poor role models use their words to belittle, negatively criticize, or constantly complain to their husbands. Any one of these behaviors will hinder, not help him.

Strength and Dignity

A wise woman has self-respect and confidence in her role as a wife. It is evident in her strength of character because she knows everything she does will reflect on her husband. She is keenly aware, of the fact, that in order for others to respect her she must first respect herself. This woman is also poised because she is fair and balanced as she represents her husband and God.

No Fear of the Future

A virtuous woman does not walk in fear because she knows what is expected of her, and she goes about her duties with her eyes focused on her purpose. She does whatever she can to plan for the future of her household. But she also knows that even though she does everything she possibly can, there are some things that are out of her control. Therefore, she follows God's leading in all that she does, and does not to worry about the end results.

Her Words Are Wise

A wise woman chooses her words carefully. There was a saying I heard when I was a child, "Sticks and stones may break my bones, but words will never hurt me." Nothing could be further from the truth. Words are powerful, and they can build up or tear down. The Bible has numerous scriptures that teach about the power of words.

It is better to dwell in the corner of the housetop, than with a brawling woman and in a wide house.
(Proverbs 25:24 KJV)

A Wise Woman Builds Her House

A soft answer turneth away wrath: but grievous words stir up anger.
(Proverbs 15:1 KJV)

The words of a man's mouth are as deep waters, and the wellspring of wisdom as a flowing brook.
(Proverbs 18:4 KJV)

What we speak is one area that wives need to pray about constantly, because most women are quick to verbalize their feelings. Often, we do not weigh our words before we speak, and this causes a lot of hurt feelings in marriages. I also know husbands fall short in this area as well. But if the wife keeps her wits about her, she can keep the enemy from disrupting the peace in her home. I know from personal experience, a lot of things we get upset about and respond to are minor. Too often, we allow the enemy to use our quick responses to bring confusion between us and our mates. This is why we need to listen when the Holy Spirit prompts us to speak or not speak. Whenever we ignore Him, it will cost us our peace.

A wise woman doesn't waste her time using words to try to prove her point. She knows the power of words and uses them to speak life and not death, blessings and not curses, peace and not confusion. A wife sets the tone in the home in many ways. She understands that her words will affect whether there will be peace or confusion in her home.

Women Standing With Their Men

Kind When Giving Instructions

It is so important that the fruit of kindness be utilized when wives ask their husbands to do something. Often, husbands and wives aren't kind to one another. They are kinder to the people they work with, or go to church with than they are with each other. Whenever a wife asks her husband to do something, her words should be thoughtful, and she should be considerate of his feelings. The virtuous woman is always gentle when she approaches her husband to ask for his help in getting something done.

Watches All That Goes On In Her Household

When a wise woman is building her house, she is aware of everything that goes on there. She knows that whatever she allows to take place will impact her family, either positively or negatively.

Not Lazy

The wife who is building her house cannot afford to be lazy, idle or slothful. She knows that being lazy will cause her house to be out of order. Husbands depend on their wives to have their home clean and organized. When a wife is lazy, she is not a blessing to her husband and has failed in her responsibility to be a helper to him.

The Scriptures tell us that when a wise woman builds her house, her children will bless her and her husband will

A Wise Woman Builds Her House

praise her. A wise Christian woman realizes the power and responsibility of the position God has given her. She must always pray for God to increase her wisdom, because life will present her with so many unexpected challenges. Her husband and children look to her to nurture them. It is a blessing when a husband and children feel home is a place where they are supported and encouraged.

In a home where there is love and understanding, family members are able to look beyond one another's faults and see their needs. The Bible tells us that, "Charity suffereth long, and is kind; charity envieth not; charity vaunteth not itself, is not puffed up, Doth not behave itself unseemly, seeketh not her own, is not easily provoked, thinketh no evil;" (1 Corinthians 13:4-5 KJV).

If Christian families would always apply this scripture in their homes, the divorce rate in Christian marriages would decrease dramatically.

Too often, Christian couples take their children to church, but fail to see that their children are affected more by what they see in the home on a daily basis, than by what they see and hear in a church service. Often, parents are fighting on their way to church, in the car. When they arrive, they put on their religious face, and sometimes resume fighting on their way home. When children observe this kind of inconsistency in the parent's behavior, it is confusing and it can weaken their faith in God.

Principle #11

A good role model for Christian wives is the virtuous woman described in Proverbs 31.

**REBELLION=CURSES
SUBMISSION=BLESSINGS**

Twelve

REBELLION BRINGS CURSES
SUBMISSION BRINGS BLESSINGS

As women of God, we have an important role in determining whether the atmosphere in our homes will be blessed or cursed. I know of too many Christian homes where the peace of God is not present. If the wife is constantly nagging her husband about something, or there is a lot of arguing and yelling, and couples are giving each other the silent treatment, that home will not be peaceful. This is especially true when the wife has not been healed from the pain she received from either childhood trauma, past relationships, or her husband. Usually, when a woman is wounded, she will respond in either quiet or open rebellion.

The Bible instructs women to be submissive to their husbands. Many wives reject the thought of submission because they feel it means becoming a doormat and loosing their individuality. Some feel that being submissive takes away their right to express their ideas and concerns.

As I touched on earlier in this book, I struggled with being submissive for years, because I had so many unresolved issues with authority figures, starting with my father. Unfortunately, he was not saved during my childhood, and he had many deep wounds of his own. Thus, when I was growing up, it appeared to me that my mother was too passive, and my father did what he pleased without any accountability to anyone. I found out later that my mother was not passive, but instead, she was passive aggressive. I was confused as a child as to how she could be saying yes to my father, but often still finding ways to do things the way she wanted to. It doesn't matter if your personality type is aggressive, passive, or passive aggressive you can still operate in rebellion.

I read a book on deliverance written by Apostle John Eckhardt, and he indicated that rebellion has many negative spirits and emotions tied to it. Some of them are greed, disobedience, lying, self-will, hate, stubbornness, evil plotting and planning, anti-submissiveness, evil control of others, destruction, resistance, deceit, friction, trickery, betrayal, false love, scorn, restlessness, sorcery, arrogance, aggressiveness, taking tranquilizers, defiance, pride, seduction, confusion, frustration, arrogance, insecurity, conniving, taking drugs, witchcraft and masculine women.

When I first read this list I could identify with it because I saw many of these traits in myself before God healed me. God used several methods to bring deliverance in my life. It took many years for me to complete the healing process. I share this because I want women who see themselves in a situation like the one I experienced to not get discouraged as they pray for God to change them. Submission will not be easy when you have unresolved issues

Rebellion=Curses, Submission=Blessings

and wounds that are still festering. But I am a living witness that God can and will heal anyone who is willing to submit themselves to Him and obey His Word. I came to realize that when I am submitting to my husband, I am pleasing God. I also discovered that submission always produces God's blessings in my home, and whatever I set my hands to do.

Do You Have A Vashti or Esther Spirit?

Vashti was the beautiful wife of Artaxerxes, king of Persia, who is known because she disobeyed her husband. At the time, her husband was the most powerful monarch in the world. The king had a great feast for the governors of his provinces. On the seventh day he commanded that Vashti be brought before him "with the royal crown" on her head, to show the people and princes her beauty. She refused to come, and she became one of the first queens in Bible history who dared to disobey her husband.

Vashti's position as queen carried with it the responsibility of being a role model for all wives. King Artaxerxes was convinced by his wise men that he should issue a new law so that other women would not be disobedient and disrespectful to their husbands the way Vashti was. Vashti was dethroned and later replaced by Esther. Vashti represents a woman with a rebellious spirit.

When a wife is rebellious, it affects her relationship with her husband negatively, and she sends the wrong messages to her children. An example of how her children could perceive her rebellion is: a daughter might feel it is acceptable to disrespect her husband, when she gets married;

a son may struggle in his relationship with his wife, if he perceives she is disrespectful to him. Some men who have had domineering mothers react by allowing their wives to dominate them and abdicate their leadership in the home. When wives are rebellious toward their husbands, they forfeit having peace in their homes.

When Vashti was dethroned, the king looked for a woman to replace her. Esther was chosen for her beauty, and because she listened to the instructions of her cousin Mordecai, who adopted her when Esther's mother and father had died. When the overseer of the king's harem saw Esther, she was given twelve months of beauty treatments and a special diet, to eat; then she was presented to the king. The king loved her more than all of the wives in his harem, and she was given the royal crown.

Mordecai had instructed Esther not to discuss her nationality with anyone in the palace, and she obeyed. There came a time when Haman, the king's right hand man, wanted to have Mordecai and all the Jews in the land killed because Mordecai refused to bow down to Haman. Mordecai asked Esther to go before the king and tell him of Haman's plan to kill all the Jews and that these were her people.

She obeyed Mordecai even though she knew she was putting her life on the line. I believe Esther was used by God because she learned submission while growing up with Mordecai, therefore, she had no problem respecting her husband as king.

Esther knew that the responsibility for the survival of her people rested on her decision. She asked everyone she knew to fast with her for three days, before she would approach the

Rebellion=Curses, Submission=Blessings

king. She did this because she knew it was a possibility that she could lose her life for coming to the king without being summoned by him. But Esther was willing to sacrifice her life for her people. Esther had a submissive spirit, therefore, the favor of God was upon her. Esther also knew she needed to fast and pray and rely upon God.

> **Then Esther bade them return Mordecai this answer, Go, gather together all the Jews that are present in Shushan, and fast ye for me, and neither eat nor drink three days, night or day: I also and my maidens will fast likewise; and so will I go in unto the king, which is not according to the law: and if I perish, I perish.**
> **(Esther 4:15-16 KJV)**

> **Now it came to pass on the third day, that Esther put on her royal apparel, and stood in the inner court of the king's house, over against the king's house: and the king sat upon his royal throne in the royal house, over against the gate of the house. And it was so, when the king saw Esther the queen standing in the court, that she obtained favour in his sight: and the king held out to Esther the golden sceptre that was in his hand. So Esther drew near, and touched the top of the sceptre.**
> **(Esther 5:1-2 KJV)**

A woman with an Esther spirit knows how to fast and pray for situations that seem to be hopeless, because she knows that she serves a God who can do the impossible. It doesn't matter what is happening in your marriage, if you fast and pray, and trust God to handle the problem. He will work things out for you and your family's good. I have had numerous experiences where I trusted God to do only what He could do. I have never been disappointed, because God is faithful. Sometimes God changes things instantly, and sometimes He just gives you the strength and peace to stand until your change comes.

Then the king asked, "What is it, Queen Esther? What is your request? Even up to half the kingdom, it will be given you."
(Esther 5:3 KJV)

When Christian wives, all over the world, begin to respond with a submissive spirit, like Queen Esther, instead of a rebellious spirit like Vashti, we will see our husbands and children and homes filled with the peace and presence of God. Then we will be the role models for women who do not know our God. I believe when unsaved women, everywhere, observe love and understanding in Christian marriages, they will begin to ask the question, "How do I get to know your God?"

Principle #12

A submissive wife is blessed and a blessing to everyone in her life.

Notes

1. William P. Barker
   Everyone in the Bible
   Pages 36, 37

2. Watchman Nee
   Spiritual Authority
   Pages 61, 62, 65

3. Steven Farmer
   The Wounded Male
   Pages 4, 11, 14

4. Dr. Myles Munroe
   Understanding the Purpose and Power of Men
   Page 28

5. Apostle John Eckhardt
   Deliverance & Spiritual Warfare Manual
   Page 42

5. All Scripture Quotations from the
   King James Version